D0842906

TICKTOCK
BANNEKER'S CLOCK

By Shana Keller and Illustrated by David C. Gardner

I'd like to thank Robyn Hardy, Robert Lett, and Gwen Marable, Benjamin's collateral descendants, along with Ralph Birt and Justine Schaeffer (director of the Benjamin Banneker Historical Park and Museum), for their support and assistance.

—*Shana*

Text Copyright © 2016 Shana Keller
Illustration Copyright © 2016 David C. Gardner
All rights reserved. No part of this book may be reproduced in any manner
without the express written consent of the publisher, except in the case of brief
excerpts in critical reviews and articles. All inquiries should be addressed to:

Sleeping Bear Press
2395 South Huron Parkway, Suite 200
Ann Arbor, MI 48104
www.sleepingbearpress.com

Printed and bound in China.

10 9 8 7 6 5

Library of Congress Cataloging-in-Publication Data

Names: Keller, Shana, 1977- | Gardner, David (David Colby), 1959- illustrator.
Title: Ticktock Banneker's clock / written by Shana Keller ; illustrated by David C. Gardner.
Description: Ann Arbor, MI : Sleeping Bear Press, [2016] | Audience: Age 6-10.
Identifiers: LCCN 2016007689 | ISBN 9781585369560
Subjects: LCSH: Banneker, Benjamin, 1731-1806. | African American
scientists—Biography—Juvenile literature | Clocks and watches—
Design and construction—Juvenile literature.
Classification: LCC QB36.B22 K45 2016 | DDC 681.1/13092—dc23
LC record available at http://lccn.loc.gov/2016007689

For Bella & Isla
I love you super much in the whole, wide, world!

S.K.

To the memory of Mary Griggs

D.G.

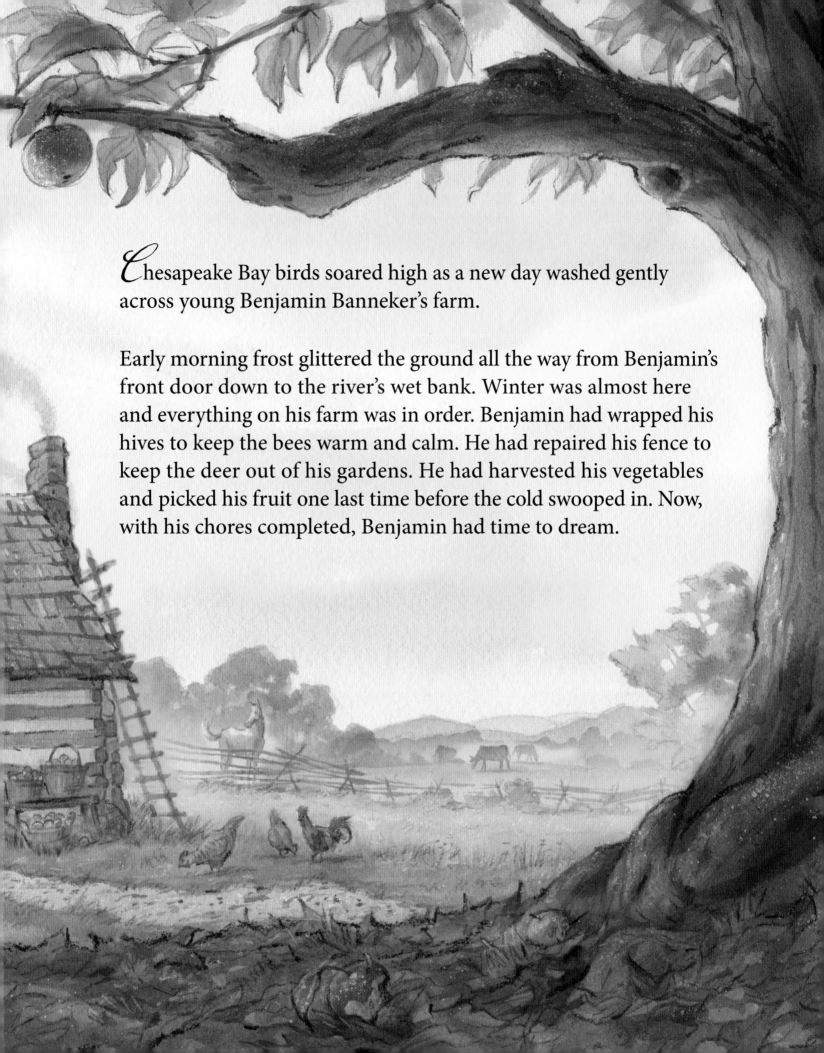

Chesapeake Bay birds soared high as a new day washed gently across young Benjamin Banneker's farm.

Early morning frost glittered the ground all the way from Benjamin's front door down to the river's wet bank. Winter was almost here and everything on his farm was in order. Benjamin had wrapped his hives to keep the bees warm and calm. He had repaired his fence to keep the deer out of his gardens. He had harvested his vegetables and picked his fruit one last time before the cold swooped in. Now, with his chores completed, Benjamin had time to dream.

Benjamin followed a familiar trail leading toward his favorite spot under the chestnut tree. For entertainment, Benjamin had taught himself how to play the violin. He had also taught himself how to play the flute. On hot summer days the tree shaded him while he played his instruments, blending his soft music with the birds' songs.

But today, sunlight danced through the bare branches as Benjamin sat down. He hardly noticed the cold ground beneath him, nor did he enjoy the beauty of the chestnut tree. Today was different. Today was quiet. He did not bring his flute or his violin to play. In his hands was a different kind of instrument, a small pocket watch.

Benjamin had borrowed the watch from a gentleman in Elkridge Landing. This was the first pocket watch he had ever seen. The gentleman knew Benjamin was clever and he was happy to share his timepiece. He trusted Benjamin and was curious to see what Benjamin could learn from a pocket watch.

Benjamin held the watch to his ear. It fascinated him. How did it work? Why was it ticking and how did the little hands move so smoothly? He knew there were gears inside it. He could hear them ticking and clicking. He thought of the gears he had seen in the mills. They were far too big to fit inside a pocket watch, of course, but the idea was the same. Gears connected together to turn things. He just didn't know how they fit exactly. Benjamin wanted to find out.

Knowing he had permission from its owner, Benjamin carefully took the case backing off the watch. Inside, he discovered a world of wonderful whirls. There were gears of all shapes and sizes. Such a tiny maze!

Benjamin took his time to study the miniature machine. This was a challenge and he loved challenges.

The timepiece was fascinating, but it was small. Too small to sit on a mantel, or hang from a wall. Benjamin knew what he wanted to do. He wanted to make a clock much bigger than the watch, one that chimed. It was called a striking clock. But how? It stood to reason: if he wanted a bigger clock, he would need bigger clock parts. But first he would need a diagram, a picture to explain how the pieces fit together.

Benjamin remembered his mathematic skills. With a proper scale, he knew he could make something big into something small, or something small into something big. Ideas swirled through his mind.

As winter rolled in and only the blue jays and cardinals remained, Benjamin carefully took the watch apart, piece by piece. In his cabin, he drew many diagrams, an exact picture of each moving part. The diagrams were needed for two reasons. The first was to make sure he would remember how to put the watch back together again! The second was to draw a bigger picture, or scale from the original, so that he could make a bigger clock.

Benjamin finally finished studying the tiny pieces. He gently put the pocket watch back together so he could return it. Then he spent the rest of the winter working on his sketches.

When the days began to lengthen and the ground was warm again, Benjamin had completed his drawings. Spring, with her bright sunny days, was the perfect time to start building his machine. There was a slight problem, however. What could he build with?

The watch was made of metal, but metal was very expensive in 1753. Benjamin did not have enough to spare for his project, nor could he afford to buy any. What could he do? What did he have? One day, while taking a break from his chores, Benjamin walked the path to his favorite spot.

Leaning against the solid tree, Benjamin worried that he might not be able to finish his project. He played his wooden flute to calm his mind. Suddenly he stopped. He looked at the land around him.

The answer was right in front of him, even in his hands! The very instrument he played was made of wood! Benjamin had plenty of wood on his farm and it was free.

Spring turned into summer. The sun was high. The garden was growing and Benjamin was excited to get started. He used every spare moment he had to find the perfect pieces of wood. Some he found by the creek, others he picked from his pear trees in the orchard.

Once he had enough wood, Benjamin began to carve the clock pieces he had drawn in his diagrams. He carved as fast as he could, but soon his excitement turned to frustration. The pieces snapped and broke. Benjamin couldn't continue to carve until he figured out why the pieces were breaking.

While he thought about his new problem, Benjamin tended his growing crops. As he was plucking bugs off his tobacco leaves a thought came to him. When his family harvested the tobacco leaves, they had to cure them. Curing meant drying the leaves out until all the moisture was gone. Suddenly Benjamin had an idea! If he could cure leaves, maybe he could cure wood. The fresh wood he used was too soft and too moist. That's why it was bending and breaking. He must dry it out to make the wood stronger!

Benjamin knew he had to be patient. Curing wood would be easy. But waiting for it to dry would take months. He picked out new pieces of wood and placed them in his family's tobacco shed. The tobacco shed was a cool, dry place, away from sunlight and away from bugs, perfect for curing. While the wood cured, Benjamin went back to work on his farm.

Finally, winter was here. Tucked under a thick blanket of snow, the farm was quiet. Harvest season had come and gone and the pieces of wood were dried out and ready to be carved.

Benjamin set out his drawings and sharpened his pocketknife. Then he began to carve.

Benjamin carved straight through the winter. He carved by the window until the sun set. When it was too dark to see, he lit his candles and carved by their light. Using his sketches, he carefully carved the large pieces and the small pieces.

He carved and carved until, finally, the pieces of wood had become parts for a clock.

By the time spring returned, Benjamin had finished carving all of the gears and wheels, and small pins he needed to hold the wheels and gears together. He had even carved large pieces into what would become the clock's stand and case.

Benjamin had every piece he needed. Every piece, except one. There was one piece he could not make from wood. The bell!

Benjamin bought his bell from a small shop in Elkridge Landing. His neighbors were excited to hear about his clock project. They couldn't wait to see it once he was finished.

With all of the clock's pieces now ready, bit by bit Benjamin began to fit everything together. He used his drawings to guide him. His toughest challenge was to get the hands on his clock to match up perfectly with the second, minute, and hour of each day. It took more than one try, but Benjamin had learned to be patient. He wouldn't give up now!

That summer, when the light was bright and warm, Benjamin set his striking clock on the mantle. Timed with the sun, he set the hands and stepped back. It worked!

When he first borrowed the pocket watch, Benjamin did not know it would take nearly two years to complete his project. But he remained focused. Over the seasons he drew his diagrams, found and cured the wood, carved the pieces, and finally assembled his clock.

The little iron bell chimed every hour, on the dot, for the next forty years. His neighbors, near and far, came to see his amazing invention.

AUTHOR'S NOTE

Benjamin Banneker was born free November 9, 1731, near what is now the town of Oella, Maryland. He lived a quiet life on a large farm with his parents, Robert and Mary Banneker, and his three younger sisters. Because he was raised in a rural area during a time of slavery, traditional school was limited to him. Whether free or enslaved, most African children in colonial America were forbidden to go to school. They were not encouraged—or even allowed—to read. However, it is noted that Benjamin, perhaps because of his status as the son of a landowner, or the kindness of his neighbors, attended elementary school for a few years. Despite the odds, Benjamin learned to read thanks to his grandmother Molly Welsh (also spelled as Mollie or Welch), from her most prized possession, the Bible.

As a young man, Benjamin would venture into town every few weeks. He purchased supplies, learned news about the colonies, and solved math problems sent to him by neighbors and farmers. Benjamin's "mental math" ability was very popular. He was often asked to help his neighbors calculate the price of goods for their crops. Eventually, Benjamin made up his own math riddles for others to solve in return. It is suspected that one of the gentlemen he traded riddles with owned the small pocket watch he used to build his striking clock.

Even after completing his amazing clock, Benjamin never stopped learning. Through books and his own observations, he studied many subjects such as science, astronomy, and engineering. Unfortunately, in 1806, several days after his death, Benjamin's cabin caught fire. All of his belongings, including the notes and journals detailing his careful observations and discoveries, were destroyed. However, several artifacts were uncovered during an excavation that pinpointed the exact location of Benjamin's cabin. These items included a bone knife handle, pottery shards, and a pipe, all of which are on display at the Benjamin Banneker Historical Park and Museum in Oella, Maryland.